TEE
HEE!

OTHER BOOKS BY S. GROSS

How Gross

I Am Blind and My Dog Is Dead

An Elephant Is Soft and Mushy

More Gross

Why Are Your Papers in Order?

Dogs Dogs Dogs

Cats Cats Cats

All You Can Eat

WITH JAMES CHARLTON

Books Books Books

TEE HEE!

A Collection of Classic Golf Cartoons

Edited by

Sam Gross

Some of the cartoons in this collection have appeared in the following periodicals
and are reprinted by permission of the authors: Diversion, El Mundo, Family Circle, Fore, Friends Magazine,
Golf Digest, Good Housekeeping, Parade, Plain Dealer, Saturday Evening Post, Scout.
Cartoons copyrighted to *The New Yorker* are indicated throughout the book.
The cartoon on page 124 by Donald Reilly is reproduced by kind permission of *Playboy* magazine.

Willow Books
William Collins Sons & Co Ltd
London · Glasgow · Sydney · Auckland
Toronto · Johannesburg

First published in the United States in 1989 as Golf Golf Golf
by Harper and Row Publishers Inc.

First published in the UK in 1990

A CIP catalogue record for this book is available from
the British Library

ISBN 0 00 218387 0

Printed and bound in Great Britain
by William Collins Sons & Co Ltd, Glasgow

"You're going to shoot
a hundred and fourteen, dear."

2

3

4

LO LINKERT

5

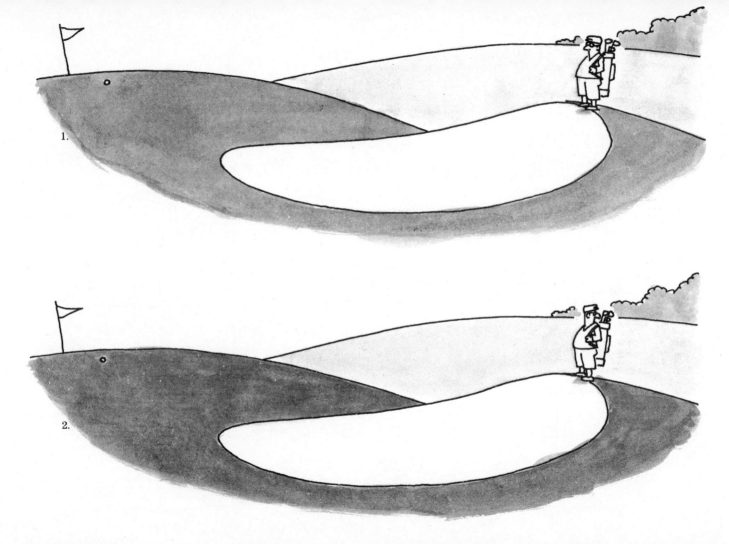

1.

2.

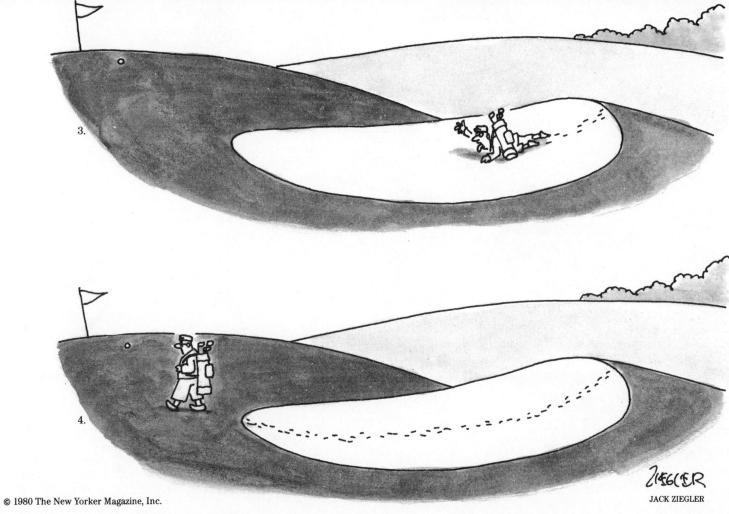

3.

4.

JACK ZIEGLER

7

"Your grip is okay, but your stance is a little wide."

"Chip's feet were cold."

ORLANDO BUSINO

9

10 "He's not having a good day. He shot his age this morning."

JOHN JONIK

"Be careful of that grass trap, Akim."

NICK DOWNES

ED FRASCINO

"I'll let you know where to send the rest of my things."

DICK OLDDEN

JOHN JONIK

14

"Teeing off early?"

In search of the missing links.

MICHAEL MASLIN

15

16

ORLANDO BUSINO

"I don't know, 'fore' hardly seems adequate."

17

ARNIE LEVIN

"Believe me, when we get back, I'm going to have a word with
the Green's Committee!"

BILL WOODMAN

19

"I wasn't talking to you. I was talking to my nine iron."

ED FRASCINO

JONIK

JOHN JONIK

Dédini

ELDON DEDINI

22

CONDOMS FOR GOLFERS

M.E. COHEN

23

"Mr. Sammett's caddie just called to say he's stuck in a sand trap on the ninth green."

MIKE TWOHY

24

"Nasty slice you've got there!"

26

FELIPE GALINDO (FEGGO)

"Every day they get a new hazard on this course."

ORLANDO BUSINO

JONIK

JOHN JONIK

David slew Goliath with a great "swing," not "sling," as previously reported.

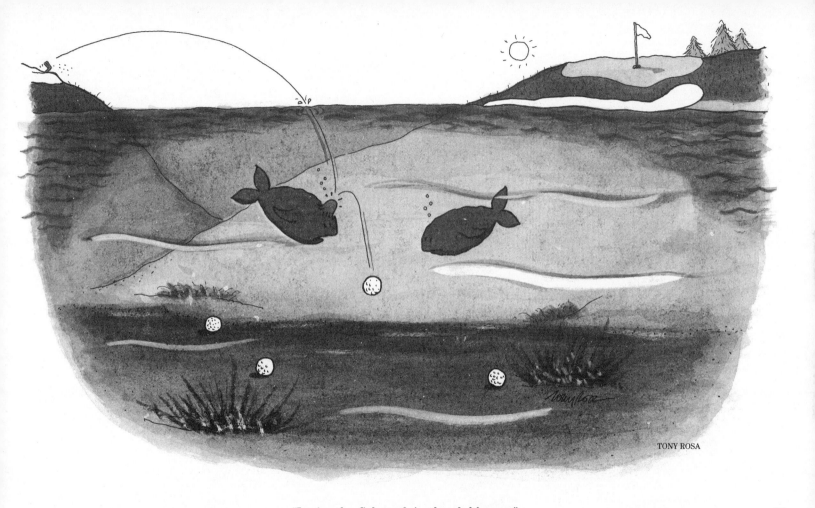

"I miss the fish tank in the clubhouse."

TONY ROSA

JERRY MARCUS

ED FRASCINO

31

DAVID JACOBSON

"I guess it's that time of year again."

33

NORT GERBERG

© 1979 The New Yorker Magazine, Inc.

"Nevertheless, I'd feel better if we played a little faster."

35

CHARLES SAUERS

"Someone with our name is winning the U.S. Open!"

HENRY MARTIN

"Do you, Helen, with a handicap of 9, take Clifford, with a handicap of 7...."

JOHN DEMPSEY

LO LINKERT

38

BILL MAUL

"The tower says your blind shot out of the woods is no more than three feet from the pin....The bad news is, the lake's only about *two* feet from the pin."

39

ELI BAUER

40

MARTY MURPHY

"—Why, yes, Mrs. Feeny—In fact, I have your file in front of me right now."

LEO CULLUM

GOLF APPAREL

"Triple bogey."

STEWART
STEWART SLOCUM

WILLIAM MAUL

© 1980 The New Yorker Magazine, Inc.

"There's no use wasting the day sulking. Why don't you get out your nice new fountain pen and write some thank-you notes?"

© 1961 The New Yorker Magazine, Inc.

"Amigos, do you mind if the Premier plays through?"

"What makes you so sure he's a hustler?"

JOHN JONIK

"Excuse me. Did you happen to see a 'Patton Penfold' skitter by?"

DON DOUGHTERTY

1.

2.

3.

JOHN DEMPSEY

"Still too much backswing. Hold your left arm
straighter. Keep your head…"

49

51

The Island of Lost Balls

REVILO

OLIVER CHRISTIANSON (REVILO)

52

"Look, I'll make you a deal. I'll get my flock to patronize your place if you get your flock to patronize my place."

MEL YAUK

53

"He's the only person to pay his membership dues on time."

Woodman

BILL WOODMAN

"What's this I hear about you giving up golf photography?"

JOHN JONIK

JERRY MARCUS

JOHN DEMPSEY

59

"That's it? 'Keep my head down?'"

JERRY MARCUS

"I can't find my life jacket."

"He got up one morning eight years ago and said he was going to take a Mulligan in the game of life. I haven't seen him since."

PORGES

PETER PORGES

"Leave my master alone!"

ARTURO POTTIER

65

66

BERNARD SCHOENBAUM

"All my life I have wondered about the river Styx. It's roughly about
a five iron, wouldn't you say?"

BRIAN SAVAGE

DICK OLDDEN

"If you knew you had to replace your divots, Herbert, why didn't you do it?"

CHARLES SAUERS

"Where did we go wrong, Alice?"

MARTY MURPHY

"It's my husband! Damn! He must have missed the cut!"

"Internal Revenue Service! Pull over!"

BRIAN SAVAGE

DICK OLDDEN

"Mind if we play through?"

CATHERINE O'NEILL

"I hope we're not going to go through this *every* time you get a hole in one."

DON OREHEK

"You would think that up here, on the last hole, they would let you keep the ball."

IF YOU CAN READ THIS YOU'RE LOOKING UP ON YOUR SHOT

BILL MAUL

JOHN CASSADY

"IV!"

"The doctor is going to give you a shot. By the time you wake up, I'll be back."

1.

2.

3.

4.

5.

6.

SERGIO ARAGONES

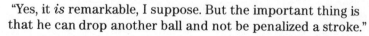
BRIAN SAVAGE

"Yes, it *is* remarkable, I suppose. But the important thing is that he can drop another ball and not be penalized a stroke."

STEWART SLOCUM

"Next!"

"Oh, for goodness' sake, forget it, Beasley. Play another one."

AARON BACALL

CHARLES SAUERS

"Happy birthday. You said you liked to shoot golf."

VAHAN SHIRVANIAN

CLEM SCALZITTI

"You've never kissed me like that!"

BRIAN SAVAGE

"I know 217 is a helluva lot for nine holes, Lou, but I also think
your caddie left a great deal to be desired."

"That reminds me....Did you pack my golf shoes?"

MARTY MURPHY

89

"Of course I can make a commitment. I'm committed to my job, I'm committed to the Constitution and I'm committed to my golf game."

JOE MIRACHI

"Thank you, God of Golf!"

AL ROSS

BERNARD SCHOENBAUM

ELDON DEDINI

"No matter *how* I treated you, Julia, haunting a man at golf is hitting below the belt."

BOOK OF
WORLD
RECORDS

SCHWADRON
HARLEY SCHWADRON

CHARLES SAXON

94

"You're getting cold."

BRIAN SAVAGE

"I thought the Supreme Court outlawed that!"

"What kind of nut would be out fishing in this weather?"

ORLANDO BUSINO

BERNARD SCHOENBAUM

AL ROSS

S. GROSS

"Beat it! I don't need a personal demon
when I'm playing golf."

97

AL ROSS

DON OREHEK

"This happens every time we pass the golf course."

99

LO LINKERT

AL ROSS

"Please, fellows! For God's sake, let me finish the hole!
I've got an *eagle* coming up!"

LO LINKERT

"I'd like golf better if they allowed a designated putter."

ARTEMIS COLE

"I'm on a golf kick. When he mentions golf, I kick him!"

"The roof, please."

JOHN JONIK

POLLS

GEORGE LEVINE

"The world's greatest invention? I'd say it was those orange golf balls."

ARTEMIS COLE

"This is for Joan Flaherty. She beat the boss at golf today."

JOHN JONIK

MANNY CURTIS

"It's a rare form of athlete's foot that only golfers get."

S. GROSS

"Remember, son, it isn't whether you win or lose, it's how you cheat at the game."

NICK DOWNES

"At least you cleared the spent-fuel pond."

CHARLES SAUERS

"Hang in there, Harry—we'll have you out of this
in no time."

MEL YAUK

BRIAN SAVAGE

"I know what you're doing back there, you filthy swine."

DON OREHEK

"I've been here since '81. I hate to think what this has done to my golf game."

JOSEPH FARRIS

BRIAN SAVAGE

"Tell me when."

ED FRASCINO

"Fair warning, Randal. I'm this close to becoming
a golf widow for real."

110

AARON BACALL

"I know it's hard for you to understand how I feel…
but you don't know the course."

ARTEMIS COLE

"You broke 100? Are you on steroids or something?"

BARNEY TOBEY

"Stop *watching* me!"

BILL MAUL

"I've heard of elevated greens before, but this is ridiculous!"

"It says that he found the game of golf inspiring at the expense
of it being relaxing."

OLDDEN

DICK OLDDEN

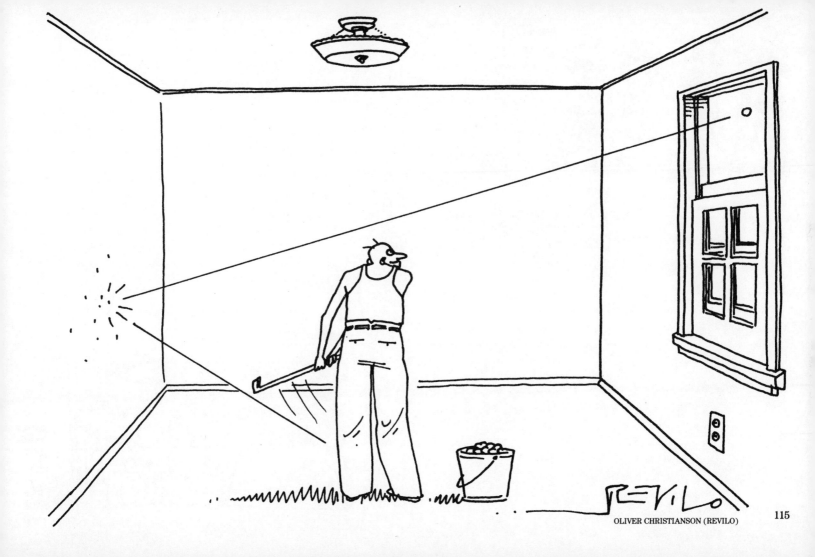

OLIVER CHRISTIANSON (REVILO)

115

ALL CADDIES REPORT IMMEDIATELY TO THE FIRST TEE!

BRIAN SAVAGE

"I'll look for the ball. You look for the club."

"I wouldn't mind her taking that much time putting, but my babysitter costs me a fortune."

LO LINKERT

ALEX NOEL WATSON

PHIL INTERLANDI

"That's Harry's problem. He's all lessons and no game."

121

GOLFBALLS THE SIZE OF HAILSTONES

JACK ZIEGLER

"A large bucket of balls and a gag!"

DON OREHEK

"Gosh, Gilliam, it's only golf."

CHARLES SAUERS

DONALD REILLY